A LONG DRAWN FACE

HOMA ZARGHAMEE

Finishing Line Press
Georgetown, Kentucky

A LONG DRAWN FACE

*for Manijeh,
a daughter, a fellow
female*

Copyright © 2018 by Homa Zarghamee
ISBN 978-1-63534-636-7 First Edition
All rights reserved under International and Pan-American Copyright Conventions.
No part of this book may be reproduced in any manner whatsoever without written permission from the publisher, except in the case of brief quotations embodied in critical articles and reviews.

ACKNOWLEDGMENTS

"Marvelous Medicine" excerpts from Roald Dahl's *George's Marvelous Medicine*
Dedication excerpt from Louise Glück's poem *"Visitors From Abroad"*

Book Design and Artwork by Emily Dawson
Artwork p. 14 by Sunny Fisher

Publisher: Leah Maines
Editor: Christen Kincaid
Cover Art: Emily Dawson
Author Photo: Carmen Campos

Printed in the USA on acid-free paper.
Order online: www.finishinglinepress.com
also available on amazon.com

Author inquiries and mail orders:
Finishing Line Press
P. O. Box 1626
Georgetown, Kentucky 40324
U. S. A.

Contents

The Son Asks	1
Two Women	2
Dolphins	4
The Letter Aitch	5
Having Fallen in Love	7
String and Bow	8
School of Fish	10
Grounding	12
Remember?	13
Toweling	14
Motherless	15
Born Post-Revolution	17
Spinning Top	18
Drawing a Face	19
As a Child of Immigrants	21
On Field Trips	22
The Occident	23
Man Best Aped	24
Late Dinner Early Breakfast	25
When Falling Asleep and Dreaming the Room	27
Deflection onto the Somatic Plane	28
Care Tips	30
Marvelous Medicine	31
The New Couple and the Wind Pollinators	32
Dear Eloise	33
Mourning and Melancholia	34

The Son Asks

I tell him the acorns underfoot when the son asks what's crunching
so with his little boot he tries
to crush one and can't
what's an acorn? an oak nut
I tell him and maybe he too
wonders why there aren't more trees
when the ground is so seed covered
and if everything that ever fell to earth wanted to
what's inside? and I stare at the riven things on the asphalt waiting
for answers to emerge he asks
me if he'll ever stop being alone
and I turn to his sister and say no
you'll be just like your mom
and tell her the acorns are empty
to forget about them
there is just she and the shedding
bark hush
just you

Two Women

She holds her
trauma in her throat
she says like swallowed
gum and so cannot
speak
and would
sooner have no words
to speak than sing
in public and would sooner
choke than go without
words

I say my throat holds
my indiscretions
and they are eager
to air
like tumblers
to the sky from standing
water

where then
is your trauma? she asks and

I show her my whole body and tell
    her as a child
        I wanted badly
            the shuttlecocks' feathers to flower
            out when I pulled them from their tube
                and I show her

            a clip of a mosquito slowly
                emerging only eyes
                    at first stretching up

                    the strength of one hundred
                        eyes tugging at war with the stagnant pond
                            for the heavy sinews of limb-wings
                            pasted taut to its sides like wet hair

                                            and I pause

                    on that prolonged tremble

            before it springs
            up and takes shape
            and I pause
            on the straining
            mosquito before its legs
            bend and take flight

and I start the video over again

Dolphins

I imagine dolphins being
the texture of tongue
a tongue developed
over the centuries
to recognize itself in the mirror
a wet photograph of a face
a wet other in the mouth
one's own tongue the only
to have been in so far
and not swallowed
until two shuffled
closer to each other
and took a car to a room
the color of seagulls
and we kissed

The Letter Aitch

My voice took on his cadence quickly
    and lingered on certain syllables
            that at first seemed random but
            emerged
                as patterned once humming through

                my own throat on their way
                to my nimble lips to be

                held there like a dogwood blossom.

    The lingering is spliced with sharp ending consonants
    the quality of a
            silent gust
                from an open window   in another room
      skimming across   the door
and slamming it shut.

It is either Loewald or Lacan who argues that
we lose a foundational piece of our souls when
we pigeonhole our mouths
        as organs of communication and forget
        how pleasurable it can be
                to suck on the candy of our own sounds.

            I bring this up lest you fear my own rhythm
            of speech subsumed
        rendered obsolete in this
        purple limerence

        that suspends my found soul
        between

    the   the
    talking   and   candy
    tree   tree

so it is a branch of both

and can never be traced
in the taxonomy of roots and grafts.

Having Fallen in Love

from the comfort of hugging
a pillow
they turn
a nagging pressure
a fascial sleeve
tugged to find
right there
me

and if my eyes are open
they see big brown eyes
and try to look
in and under
for stirrings of life
and then even deeper
as if my eyes can be
tunneled

I welcome the burrowing
I know there's no other way
to a heart
even if it's not mine
they push toward
and the time
comes when they recoil
from the openness
and ask why
are they open

we can wait for winter
I respond
when marshes freeze dusted
over with enough ice chip
or snow to give a clear view down
to what belongs
to earth
the grasses the ferns the elders
but to obscure reflection

String and Bow

    untuned words came out of you
    and instead of disbanding into white noise
      they condensed in me
    like a leaky faucet
        to a percussive drip

            you knew intuitively you said that
              I would always annoy you and
              you would eventually hurt me
      always annoy
             eventually hurt
                    always annoy

                    eventually hurt

now on a bench staring at a river
you drown those words in a new movement:
    winds

a well-aimed exhalation in my ear interrupts and I try
to chew what I was saying
      back into the words
           gummed up in my cheek
to taste the last of my thoughts before your breath
before the tremble of its hum
    hum as thin as the hair you move out of the way
        to suspend your nose at my ear's notch
        as you had once suspended it at the cusp
            of thighs saying
                how good I smell
                in accusation   almost
                before saying my body is almost
        perfect   and the percussion
                          of "almost"
                          fades in

and it's that hair I feel now
        the whole length of it back and forth
        not moved off but in
                held taut at my ear and lowered to that other verge
                where another you bites the hair's end
                and shakes his bared teeth from side to side
        and I see this
is how you make music

School of Fish

I.

let me reach
down into my
feelings pulled low
by gravity like blinds
like my tears he
always told me
fell in the straightest
lines like anchor rope

II.

from land
waves are
ripples nothing more
than wet wrinkles
but submerged
there's violence
and treading and truth
to his statement
that he's never seen me
joyous and just
because he never looked
doesn't mean he's not right

III.

the fish react
to the surge with dignity
a standing still a
patience in letting
it pass a coolness
a camouflage
to aspire to
if you learn to hold still
they wink
then you can swim
for hours with the tide
until it exhales
and calms and finally
feels through absence
its foregone agitation
and ascribes to its own
force any wriggling you
might have got caught in

Grounding

An angel faints off a cloud
and floats down from side to side
tracing out an evergreen silhouette
to finally approach earth laterally
like a blown parachute

pinning small feathers
from my belly button
as I dig for lint it seems
right I'm a pillow but unfair
my head can't find a place to rest

so it funnels into my neck's
dim alley said to open out to the heart's
piazza where supposedly
the celebration is constant
no matter the mood stoned
into the surrounding walls
or fibered into the coverlet's down

Remember?

When dandelions were
yellow first and then froze
into exquisite moth
embroideries an exhalation could
shatter
fast as a forehead
blowing against a windshield
and not the other way
around?

                The forehead does
                   not breathe in

                                  Chicken wire is
                         was and has always been sold
                          in rolls and only unrolled
                            to keep chickens
                                      in
                              not the other
                               way around

                                Now as snakes age
                          synovial honey not sweat
                      leaks from their pores because
                           they have no armpits
                           and when it all
                   glistens out like sunfire
under the garden's visiting hours
                                  they freeze
                         into dusty dandelion
                     cloth tangled around
                     their caterpillar souls
and even those softest of soft
                                      souls
                              melt away
                            in the thaw
                   before an angle emerges

Toweling

She cannot see
her body in her
floorfallen clothes
but she is sure
it must have once
been there.
When her head
hangs over the
bathtub the traces
she brushes
just out of sight
trickle from her
so she can count them
uncountable
until they have
landed
invisible
as they are
in air.

Motherless

I.

To feel motherless means no
assumed observer and what
would the earth do
if the moon looked away
into the void
instead
or worse
at the sun
at the stars
would the womb
cave in?

She feels motherless and it feels
like the inside of her skin
is shaved so nerves and sinew
tendons and whatever attaches
muscle and fat are severed
and her skin is suspended around her
as a halo around
the moon.

II.

Cut hair falls to the floor
a tipped glass puddles
and she lets it
                                  in
                                                        an exploratory spirit
                    to see if
        wet
                                                      the cut hair crawls

and ivies itself
            into a crown
                                        or knot.

Born Post-Revolution

please excuse the daughter's
appearance she wasn't even
there but she's been in a state
of shock since
something about adrenaline
response to furniture flung
from windows and millions
chanting God's greatness
by rooftop each night
no electricity that winter and milk
warmed between mother's
and grandmother's thighs yes
of course people too not just
furniture and yes windows
the home and home
the country the continent
the chanting soured
a few months after to nothing
more than petrified crickets
when her arms stayed long
from reaching for hugs
from distracted people

Spinning Top

I find a spinning top
wooden and drawn
on it with marker and shaky
hand is a spiral so when
it spins it hypnotizes
with cartoonish insanity
the eyes gazing down at it
and when it is still I remember
the coffee quaking this morning
as my father lowered
it to the breakfast table
a hand-me down
from a friend's hoarding
mother who expired
the day I moved to a larger
space that accommodates
heavy furniture and appliances
years of toilet paper and detergent
salt and pancake mix I stir together
like the solar system of a tired god
watching the spoon's trail run around
like time in heat like the numbered
neighborhoods of a remote city
where youth tried to sniff
drugs off sand
to sift itself from beauty
and beauty from love
so that alone it might
have a chance at lasting
while the top
on the living room sofa
is propelled into motion by my mother
watching her unlived lives
and on the train now
I close it in my palms
instead of revealing to the eyes above
it has been spinning here this whole
time under the dark of my fingers

Drawing a Face

I started with the eyes
then contoured the head's shape
and filled it with the cheeks
nose
forehead
chin
my mother
told me it's perfect
my father said wow
a closed mouth is lips
an open mouth gums
tongue
palate
inner cheek
subtle differences so easily exaggerated
teeth
each tooth's outline
so easily overdone
most difficult is the hollow that's none of these
its depth
different textures
different shades of black
reflecting the surrounding structures
well you started strong but you ruined it
my father
my mother
I know how to fix it
I'll show you tomorrow
a teacher once told us
we can always see in a drawing
where the artist struggled
flow
and its lack
are not just attributes of process
but result
the next day

my mother said
I hope you won't be upset with me
but I went ahead and did it myself
my point is not that
effortlessness cannot be a product of effort
my point is I struggled to draw an open mouth
and my mother drew it
perfectly
closed

As a Child of Immigrants

I watch rain wash solid matter

of smaller solid matter
and fluidly conceive of the pitter
pattering darts down any surface's
hard plane to be both banshee dash
and midnight raid scaring
up debris in their rush

rain moves rain rakes rain expatriates

                I watch rain wash air
              of detritus suspended aloft
          in its new element paralyzed
       lost and upended splintered almost
         to the point of invisibility and
          only see this stubborn clue
           as hovering color refusing
             to be seen through

                          so that by the time rain finally intervenes

                                    it is the raindrop
                        that by braving being dissolved
                            into by a foreign body
                      has demonstrated its humanity
                          nobility vim and vigor
                    and fogged the true nature
                              of its operation
                      that when it falls down

                                  it cleans up like a
                                      gravedigger

On Field Trips

in my northeastern township
we rubbed the long side
of crayons on shelf paper
held to the grave of the unknown
soldier while a man with prominent
shoe buckles and pilgrim hat
claimed to resemble
our forefathers and I tried to picture
my grandmother among these pacing
turkeys but could see only a kiss
on the locked lattice of Imam Ali's
glittering tomb and the time
in the Worlds of Fun roller coaster
queue when a man in shorts
asked what we were
speaking and how to say
Jesus loves you in Farsi

The Occident

one man
cuts eyeholes
in a draped bedsheet
to rape
one man
hides in raindrops
streaking down a leaky roof
to impregnate
a lucky virgin
so fortunate she thinks
gazing at her son
to have the perfect boy
who washes
before his last meal
men's feet
how well worth his slow death
that his lover must watch and weep
on the books
for all time
a whore

Man Best Aped

waterfall with car wash
sunset with shutters
broccoli with H bomb

and spring with runoff
from an East Village
window-unit AC

And the Height

of human creativity
was supplanting
thumb for mother's breast
and creating God
for the loss

Late Dinner Early Breakfast

To mince one must learn
to reconstitute the whole
from lengthwise cuts
then to cut across
as thin as possible

or one can crush
in one gesture as a cockroach
under a shoe and feel the pop
of the soul bursting out
as if bombed when life becomes
an outward dissolution
as when my father said
I could see in black holes
the back of my own head
and I pictured at the time
translucent organs
as if cooled beyond ice
now I envision a vacuum
emptying before me
the contents of my mind
and my heart has moved
to my foot where I crack
it bone by bone
remembering the cockroach
and *where id was*
ego shall be where shrapnel
explodes out so it is blade
not hallucination not a cloud
but a precise ray yes life:
some metal shards drawn
if deranged enough
to the human magnet

the knife unwashed tastes
of garlic on morning pear
all of which my stomach
makes of dying ice cubes
in a tumbler and my eyes try
to organize the newspaper's
ungrammatical world
as other than end times

When Falling Asleep and Dreaming the Room

I.

through the slight slits
the eyes maintain
in even the tarriest
sleep leaks in
the room:

    the limbs reaching out
    from the cranial
    floor plant

        the scarf cloaked over and down
        the neck from the bedside
        lamp's face

            the silhouette of the overcoat
            draped across the heavy shoulders
            of the desk chair

II.

the fencer's
mask and confronted
with such targeted attention
depending on the scarf
jousting and buzzing
his invisible stare
set into motion
around a tentacle
and constricted
grip
its covered eyes
see and again in case
and concluded
under there
hands

mask was a beekeeper's
the hunched woman
that she took turns
as dueler and bee
around her antagonist
and she was perforce
as the ocean
somehow both flung
by the fingerless
needling it once for fear
moved where she could not
they were still
there must be hands
not muscles

Deflection onto the Somatic Plane

when my plant task
in bed is to grow
sleep

the seemingly
healthy melon caves
in exposes

not soft
flesh not mold
but a system

of stalactite and stalagmite
ossified in escape
in attempts at airing

or a system of machine
teeth grinding
and churning teeth

powered by lack
of lamplight
and souring

life force loverless
libido fatherless aggression
now trying

to remember specifics
of the fish
the sarcastic fringehead

fish
so that I can
convince you I am not

the first animal
there is precedence
in nature

for opening the mouth
wide and fighting
with kisses

Care Tips

The widow's response may be to dig
the sidewalk for three days,
to lay pavers and hug
fifty-pound bags of gravel
sliced open at the bottom
until they are empty,
to wait for rain.

She may throw you a trowel
and ask you to turn
the soil, to plant new seeds,
calling you Agent Sunflower each time
she meets your cautious gaze.
You may be alarmed at all the rocks
that crumble in your palm.

Marvelous Medicine

The last time you saw him
after chemo was abandoned
and the widow hung a pitcher plant
and their home became hospice
and their bed became what it is
she may have fetched his favorite children's books.

Reading to them the tale
of a boy attempting to purge
his grandmother of grouchiness,
you may have found yourself saying aloud
> *the whole point of medicine, surely,*
> *was to make a person better. If it didn't*
> *do that, then it was quite useless,*

speaking of
> *a new medicine,*
> *one that is so strong*
> *so fierce and so fantastic*
> *it will either cure her completely*
> *or blow off the top of her head.*

It may have been unbearable
that the grandmother's
problem with the boy
was that he grew too fast.
She may have told the boy
> *Never grow up…Always down.*

This may be what comes to mind
when you pick up the bag
of his ashes and ask the widow
for a scale to compare the weight
to his birth.

The New Couple and the Wind Pollinators

I.

This condition
a body's foolish plea
to find in new love
the last.
How does she ask
new love for help?
Help to make new
love old?

II.

As spring gusted in
he made her promise
she would love again
and by summer
the widow did.

III.

They study
the monkey puzzle
spine from limb
and linger too long
on what is clear to see
this young conifer
is neither redwood
nor sequoia.

Dear Eloise

if you wear a blonde wig
and smile at me
with chattering teeth
I'll recognize you
as myself a continent over
a burn victim
not in a conventional sense
they tell me
your chest is a landscape
moldering and now in your brain
the dust mites have settled
on the spot where language lives
so God himself will have to blow on
the French books Italian English
to hear your voice always
said to be an angel's

Mourning and Melancholia

Alive
they had shadows, dead
they glow.

I reason: where I glow,
where I am lit by their death halations,
hit and run, blood cancer, plane crash, aneurysm,
these parts of mine must
also be dead.

I reason: proceed, mourn,
then, Homa. Mourn these most
brightly lit parts. Mourn crossing
the street, you will stay on one side now,
mourn headlights approaching, their growing stare,
they're not stars but hellfire now, missiles and bombs.
Mourn your New York calculations of prancing footwork
against traffic lights and barreling steel, you have no more feet,
all lights are red. Mourn green and yellow and white. Mourn
your body's three dimensionality, mourn what was not
mowed down, mourn standing up and breathing out,
mourn depth, you are flat now, 2D.

Mourn your height, tall girl,
mourn a solid standing spine,
mourn structural integrity. Mourn
blood you can trust, blood that can live
side by side with your bones. Just mourn all
your blood, fluid blood, liquid blood, mourn the red life
streaming in your veins. Your blood is now a bag of glass that cuts you
when you move, cuts when it's shook. Your blood is an axe, a grinding
axe at the base of your spine, sharpening to cut you down.
Mourn the tree, you're a stump. Mourn your
tall youth, you're shrinking
like a hunchback, short
and getting shorter.

Mourn flying,
Homa bird, mourn your
ancient name, it couldn't save you,
mourn your golden wings, your myth, your foreshadowing
of kings, mourn your endless legless flight, your never landing,
mourn your freedom, your charge to execute any who try to cage you alive.
Mourn flight itself, mourn the sky, the clumsy sky that dropped a prince in
the sea. Mourn the foreshadowed kings and the crowns, mourn your power
over them, mourn them mattering so much less to you than you to them,
mourn nothing weighing upon you. Mourn each of the forty nights
that count out the execution of your cager, bird. Mourn the bird,
it's over. You never had legs, now
you don't have wings.

Mourn tight vessels
in your brain. Mourn the wand
before the bubble was blown, mourn
a brain so strong it blew a bubble without a peep,
a silent bubble, undetected bubble. Mourn the blown bubble,
glowing like the moon, both shadow and bright, mourn clarity with chrome,
every oily color, mourn soft and spirited changing hues, mourn reflections,
bending light. Mourn the bubble itself.
It did what bubbles do.

Homa Zarghamee is a behavioral and experimental economist and professor of economics at Barnard College. Her research uses psychological insights to understand economic phenomena. She received her Ph.D. and M.A. in Economics and B.A. in Mathematics and Economics from Cornell University. She is also an affiliate scholar at Columbia's Center for Psychoanalytic Training and a visitor at the Santa Fe Institute.

www.ingramcontent.com/pod-product-compliance
Lightning Source LLC
LaVergne TN
LVHW041551070426
835507LV00011B/1040